THEOPOETICA:

An Anthology

Charli Pence Bond
Ethan Nosanow Levin
Abigail Grace Louisin
Jason Adam Sheets

APRIL GLOAMING

Edited by:

Emma Peterson Cardiel & Robyn Leigh Lear

Publisher's Cataloguing-in-Publication Data

Bond, Charlie Pence; Levin, Ethan Nosanow; Louisin, Abigail
Grace; Sheets, Jason Adam
    Theopoetica: Divine introspections / written by Charli Pence
    Bond, Ethan Nosanow Levin, Abigail Grace Louisin, & Jason
    Adam Sheets
    ISBN: 978-1-953932-11-2

1. Poetry: General 2. Poetry: American - General 3. Poetry:
Jewish I. Title II. Author

Library of Congress Control Number: 2022934918

CONTENTS

CONTENTS

∶

Ethan Nosanow Levin

CONTENTS

∴

Abigail Grace Louisin

CONTENTS

::

Jason Adam Sheets

Preface

Emma Peterson Cardiel &
Robyn Leigh Lear

"He who is subjected to a field of visibility, and who knows it, assumes responsibility for the constraints of power; he makes them play spontaneously upon himself; he inscribes in himself the power relation in which he simultaneously plays both roles; he becomes the principle of his own subjection."

– Michel Foucault, "Discipline and Punish"

"In Buddhist philosophy, the deva, Indra, is said to have cast an infinite net. A multi-faced jewel is embedded in each vertex of this woven matrix, jewels so magnificent and polished that they possess perfect reflection. As one gazes upon any particular gem, they would see every other reflected within it, an endless multitude of glittering images, each a representation of the unfathomable Other. Within its original conception, this metaphor seeks to establish a metaphysical interconnection; we both project outward at the Other and cannot help but absorb the projections cast at us. We are a composite, a conceptual Frankenstein that unconsciously repurposes and redirects into each other. We are a singular multitude."

– Michael Brandon Stoddard, "The Pandemic Panopticon"

Theopoetica: An Anthology manifested in our catalogue after a conversation with Jason Adam Sheets, and it was received by our editorial staff with great reverence and anxiety. As a press who looks to unpack the strangeness of the stigmatized and perceived ignorance our racial and religious past defines us by, even now, there was some fear in adding this to our communal canon. When we initially read *Theopoetica*, we grappled with how the work contributed to the central mission we all have embarked on in this language and visual art collective turned publisher, turned away from religiosity, turned back to each other to see into the eyes of our collective strangeness. It was then we reread the manuscript and realized these four guides turned to poetry to turn back to one another in conversation. The works echoed a sameness that we Southerners have lived for generations. This is that these works choose to live and converse and be changed by being bound together. No one voice is giving prominence over another. We Southerners are bound together more tightly than many who live outside the South realize, and so our conversations are too. We do not have the luxury of escaping each other because many of us will never know the freedom capital and wealth and advanced education can grant. We live with our ghosts and our neighbors in the South, and we feel each other's pains, and we hate each other because the mirror is too real to stare into at times, but we make meals too big for our families to give to those who are hungry. So, if we can do it, so can those who are gifted with the platform that echoes past the echo chamber of ourselves.

So, we read *Theopoetica* again and again since it did not fit our perceived formula until the small, tattered edge of the veil was lifted for us, lasting maybe only a second. We do an unbelievable amount of searching for the answer when it sits right in front of us (don't we all?). *Theopoetica* is a unique lesson in differences and the importance of recognizing how we process difficult times through difficult texts.

At April Gloaming, we aim to reclaim what it means to be Southern. Part of our personal definition of reclamation is making space to understand people and not isolate them. In *Theopoetica*, the reader hears the voices of people overlooked who are finally taking up space and creating a new definition to be added to the ever-growing complex haunt in the South. In these voices, we hear the mistakes of our ancestors and the mistakes we must work toward repairing—young children silenced by expectations and people expelled from their homelands explained in stories returned to us in our daydreams and discussions. We learned of empty, hurting spaces both inside and outside ourselves. However, the discussion of pain has the ability to act as a soothing balm. *Theopoetica* highlights failures made before us, but, by making space for the acknowledgment of these injustices, it gives us the ability to take steps toward mending.

The decade of the 2020s started with major loss and strife, and it continues as the pandemic separates families and friends, both politically and physically. Fear has driven our decisions and divisions; now, we need reminders of our sameness. In *Theopoetica*, each poet tells distinct stories, and we are confronted with our own losses. Whether it is loss of relationship or culture, these authors speak into collective wounds. We enter a world of perceived self-doubt and questioning with Charli Pence Bond and Abigail Grace Louisin, where we can see the battle within ourselves as a woman and a child. Ethan Nosanow Levin brings us into a space where we face losses larger than ourselves and are left questioning "how." Ultimately, Jason Adam Sheets ends the collection on a theme of loneliness all-consuming as the sea, where we all have sat during past months of quarantine and social limitation. There is connection in suffering, and these poets have composed a work reminding us of our sameness. Abigail Grace Louisin summarizes my sentiment by stating, "I cannot separate my sadness from yours...Cruelty, after all, is made of distance".

As editors, we too have to acknowledge the special privilege seeing beginning drafts of inner thoughts and feelings on the page and take heed in knowing the magnitudinous role the critic plays in shaping futures. Our suggestions and critiques are either taken or cut, but the essence of the original art always stays. Writing is an artform that projects internal emotion outward, and we realize we are not alone. Metaphorically, we do not light the fire, but we set it to burn universally bright against the night of our past. Art pushes us to burn, to live, to test, and to grow from the burning, or to quote Sheets, art asks us to, "look out of the window's windowglass...carrying with it a story that begends...dissolved in the eye of some living thing." In *Theopoetica*, the poets actively engage with hard topics that contradict at times. This dissension creates a space where questions exists but are not written and encourages the reader toward personal growth and reflection. A whispered demand for it like holy fire burning. In the end, it was an honor to edit this collection, and we look forward to seeing how this work is consumed by readers. We hope its insights can give you at least an inkling of self-discovery and churn the current of your ever-deepening sight the way it did ours when we nurtured the poetic ritual that manifests while reading these pages from these spirit(ed) poets.

Introduction

Ethan Nosanow Levin

*"The whole business of writing is the question of living contempo-
rariness [one's] contemporariness .... The thing that is important
is that nobody knows what the contemporariness is. In other words,
they don't know where they are going, but they are on their way."*
– Gertrude Stein, "How Writing is Written"

An Animist, a Christian with strong Catholic roots, an
Evangelical, and a Jew enter a Zoom room. It sounds like the
beginning of a bad joke. But this is the origin of *Theopoetica:
An Anthology*. The authors of this volume first gathered in a
course titled "A Poetics of Difficulty" in the Fall of 2020. It was
taught by Professor Amy Hollywood under the spiritual auspic-
es of Harvard Divinity School. The course asked the question:
"What does it mean to read difficult texts in difficult times?"
This was too fitting for the first full semester of remote learning
during the pandemic. Through the exploration of experimental,
innovative, and "avant-garde" ¬¬writing, we were charged to
navigate the modalities of difficulty: "What kinds of difficulty
are there? Which are useful to think and sit with, to feel through
– and which perhaps are not? And how does the difficulty of the
contemporary world, in all of its particularity, require difficult
writing – even as it might also require other things too?"
From our four divergent perspectives, the authors of this
collection began to share with each other original poetry which
reacted to the difficulty of our assigned readings and to the hard-
ships of our own lives. What started as a central academic and
poetic pursuit, ultimately manifested into the work before you.

It was an unexpected blessing to create in the midst of a multi-faceted struggle: a struggle with texts, with each other, and with the dehumanizing affects emanating from the blue light of our computer screens during a global pandemic.

Gertrude Stein in the quote above calls for living contemporariness in the act of writing, and the contemporary moment is theological in proportion. The pandemic is a hellish disaster; divine in its scientific complexity and godly in its capacity to bring the subjective to a boil. But the theos of this pandemic, the divine which manifests both as mercy and stern judgement, cannot be captured through the rational instruments of theology. The logos does not see the contemporariness of this theos in writing. Its truth lies beyond the threshold of interdisciplinary study. The contemporariness of the pandemic rests instead in the realm of the poesis, in the unfolding process of its creation. This is the function and purpose of a theopoetica: to bear witness to the lifting of the veil in a moment of inexplicable harm. No one knows what is beyond the veil, but its witness may be a path toward healing.

Each author paints a different shade of the movement inherent in the method of theopoetica. Despite our context as divinity school students, the appeals to classical religion are far and few between, except perhaps in my own work. I consider it as much a form of modern midrash, of myth bathed in neon light. Many a traditional Jewish text comes alive for me in these pages. Charli's verse seems at a glance to masquerade as prose. The sentences are condensed and the grammar exact. But underneath the taught aesthetic sits layers of depth, revealing in a moment, for instance, how pig tails tied too tight signifies both the rupture of space and condensation of time. Abigail's poetry is a lesson in memory and its commitments to splashes of color on the canvas of the page. Never again will charcoal and gold raise in you such raw emotions. Her work draws you into the page; you become the words & feel their flowing. Jason is the most seasoned poet of the bunch, and his gentle demeanor gave us all guidance in the painful process of producing this work. Read out loud his writing and hear it ring beyond the confines of its exquisite construction and into the realm of pure sound and meaning. Play in his words, find the magic of the nature it reveals below the layer of concrete. Take in each author as an individual and consider us together. The final product is ultimately yours.

We present to you Theopoetica: Divine Introspections. Encounter it in due process.

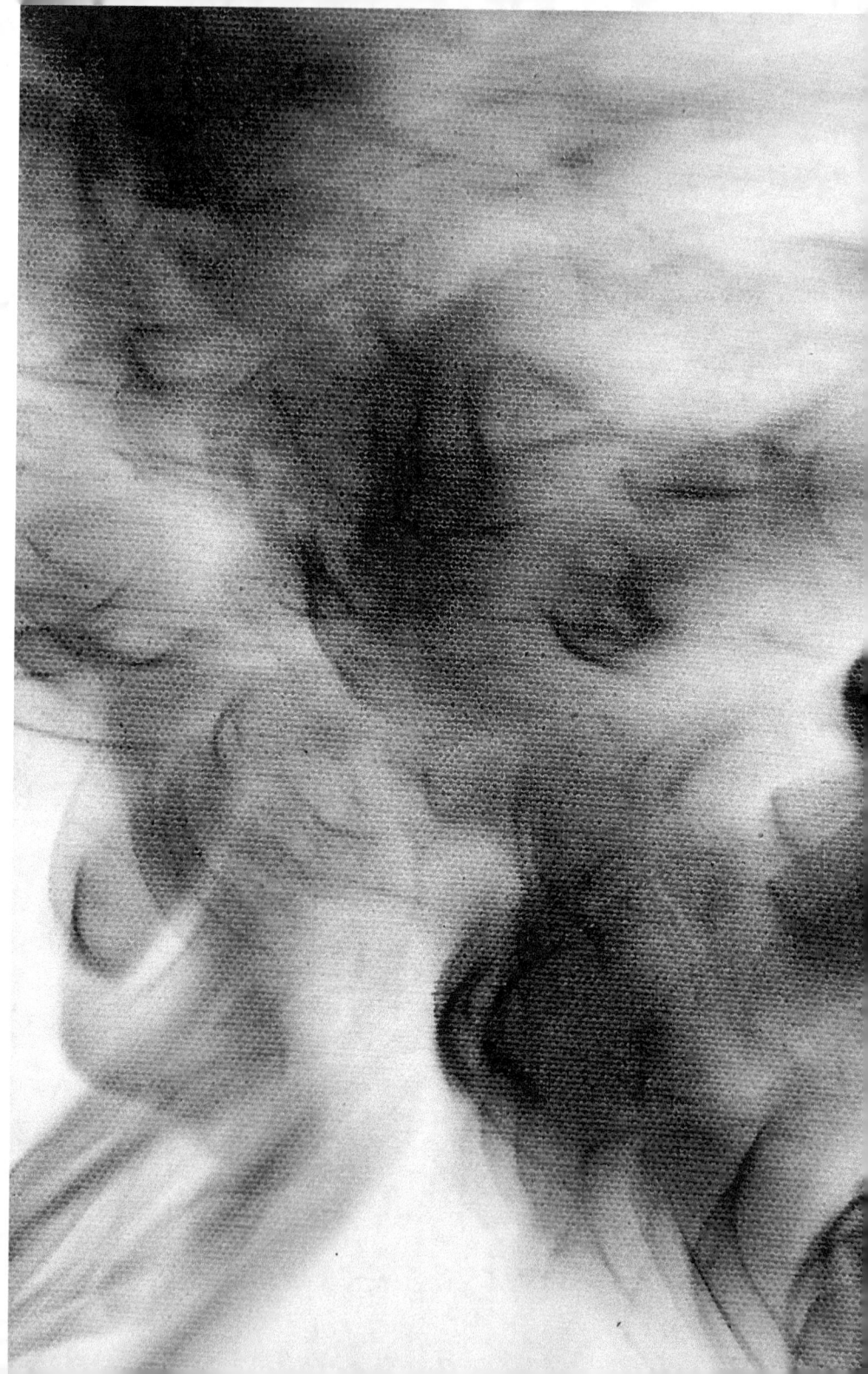

·　Charli Pence Bond　·

10.13.20

an "undiscovered country" linked to each of us
names continuing a genealogy and I wonder if a part
is the places we seek

names are part substance—part what we make them
when you name a child you declare something over her
you tell her what she is going to be, what she is capable of being

so what does a name shout
is it a pattern of symbols and syllables
do some sound nice and others ugly—why

why do I hear your name in the train echoes
rolling behind our neighborhood at night
wishing it were closer so it would wake me

10.19.20

The little boy is unsure
if the ant really is the strongest
in the world.

He leans down to watch
them hurry, barks orders
but still isn't sure.

How they pass the time.

They are strong and fit, yes.
What makes their labor full.

He starts to hum:

>   teaches them the words
>   so they can sing too
>   while they work
>   while they run
>   while they defend the homeland
>
>   And soldier on.

Let someone else sing for a while.
The young woman is unsure when they say she is the strongest
    in the world.

10.26.20

dead beach roam groom fall fail filter
who thought these legs couldn't run

independent
in dependents
with the dependent, a dent.
and this dent fills with something, not water, but it drowns.
and waits.
and wonders.
and watches.
and feels, no, not that, doesn't do that;

pick please sort stack put away then soar today
is it better to launch into the sunset or ride off to the rise of day

where the bird lands on the boat and stops,
waits, doesn't sing this time,
it's metal loud no air but sticky soap on the sides &
machines that go into the sky
who thought those wings couldn't fly

squints a little, tilts head to one side;
which way does the wind blow?
he taught me how to tell but I forgot.

II.9.20

keeping close—making sense—wondering what there might be
in the spaces under wooden planks of porches;
they creak when she walks on top of them
they don't break—just bend—she rocks back and forth,
standing on the edge, holes in socks invite damp air on her skin.

keeps looking out over the fields, down the lane,
asking him to come back and knowing he
won't, but mom still put her hair in pig tails too tight just in case.
her scalp strains against the tension but she doesn't take them out yet,
no, not until the fireflies peek out before the sun sets.

keeps glowing, she likes the ones that shine early, they know their spark
will be insignificant in the fading sunlight, and she wonders if they
are always there, taking flight even in the morning, their contribution
invisible in the light of day.

II.I7.2O

If she is good at singing, must she?
The notes move to try to follow her
down town—to the spot outside

where there is a hole in the wall to a valley,
canyons of girls eating, so easy,
skip to the end, no friends,
if only songs could face them now;
ace it loud, what are you winning,
why aren't you singing;

she is keeping it open, just straighten your mind
but there are mirrors on this side, the fun house kind,
keep moving, eyes on the ground,
sing again, sing loud again,
tune out their sounds
        reminding you it's better when there are crumbs
        in the bag
        and less to grab.

your body is dust gathering,
they are gathering dust;
if she is saved by singing,
we must.

II.23.20

you couldn't write a poem
because the voice didn't work
when the air paused;

it was only for one second,
the answers stilled,
and time broke
when the voice it stopped working.

no response comes,
but who were you even asking;
did you want to hear from God or him;

a strong thump in your mind or head and it's
telling your heart it should feel sick,
and so it did;
and so you quit the asking;

but then a motion, a sift of the eyelid in a coma,
a thread of light within a storm,
a shout from the shore,
a reason to believe he can still hear;

the night sky makes you feel close to him,
those stars, she said, stretch out and grab them,
but what if you can't;
still try, one more time,

maybe he can reach them —
when above black ocean
he hovers,
turns off lights and whispers
to those secret universes,
and thinks of telling you.

II.30.20

Each day I watch him leave,
turn back to the small ears
who don't know what it means,
tell them he will be home soon,
don't follow the rules   keep coloring,
turn back to the small voices on the news
who don't know why he goes,
turn to retreat   stop   wait

There is a sprout in the ground
where she buried the sunflower
seeds last week, they got stuck
in his teeth and she giggled
and pushed hers down

deep into the soft soil
a blanket for their sleep;

12.4.20

everyone is a failed something
        cs lewis wanted to be a poet

you're not supposed to say that word in a poem
or that one either, but hold fast

don't let the gas run out of the mast
there's more to the land up ahead

keep your eyes open and up your head
don't let the walls fall down, they're all we have

broken in thirds, fourths, halves,
sliced thin she is and she does

but there will always be just because
and what people mean by the olive branch she finally knew:

the secret is the hand that holds it out belongs to you.
        everyone is a failed something.

12.4.20 (2)

licks the envelope, isn't allowed anymore
presses it to her forehead before
she takes a bite out of the heart of the matter
they say it that way as if there is only one center,
there are many, circling her, watching,
the foxes gather outside planning their attack,
first coffee, a list of talking points before they go live,
don't declare what you feel the poison to be,
just take a sip,
we promise we will make it go away,
we will go make it away,
will you go make it this way,
away you go
make a will and a way
we will make a way
we don't go
away

12.1.20

her bees will stay
feed the flowers, keep them going,
appreciate the ones planted for them.
They have a home here, yet winds decide
where they flit, they promise her to keep it up,
hunting for the perfect piece
moving toiling sweating
coming home from a long day,
put their feet up and hold hands
after dinner by the fire,
picking a television show is always a task
then it's too late and off to bed again,
turn off the lights and know
that tomorrow's work still means something,
even unseen,
they did their best, do their best, now rest;
i love you, goodnight,
ignore those outside,
        eyeing the hive

NOTES

"10.13.20"

The quote, "undiscovered country," references Susan Howe's poem, "Since," from Concordance, p. 20.

"10.19.20"

Proverbs 30:24-25

"10.20.20" & "10.26.20"

This poetry is inspired by the collection "Arrows" by Dan Beachy-Quick

"11.17.20"

The "dust" is inspired by Caroline Bergvall's "Drift"

"11.30.20"

The "Doomstead Days" collection by Brian Teare inspired the use of seeds in the poetry.

"12.4.20"

The structure of this poem was inspired by "Duplex" poems in Jericho Brown's "The Tradition." The wordplay in this poem is inspired by Caroline Bergvall's "Drift."

"12.4.20 (2)"

The wordplay in this poem is inspired by Caroline Bergvall's "Drift" and the collection "Arrows" by Dan Beachy-Quick.

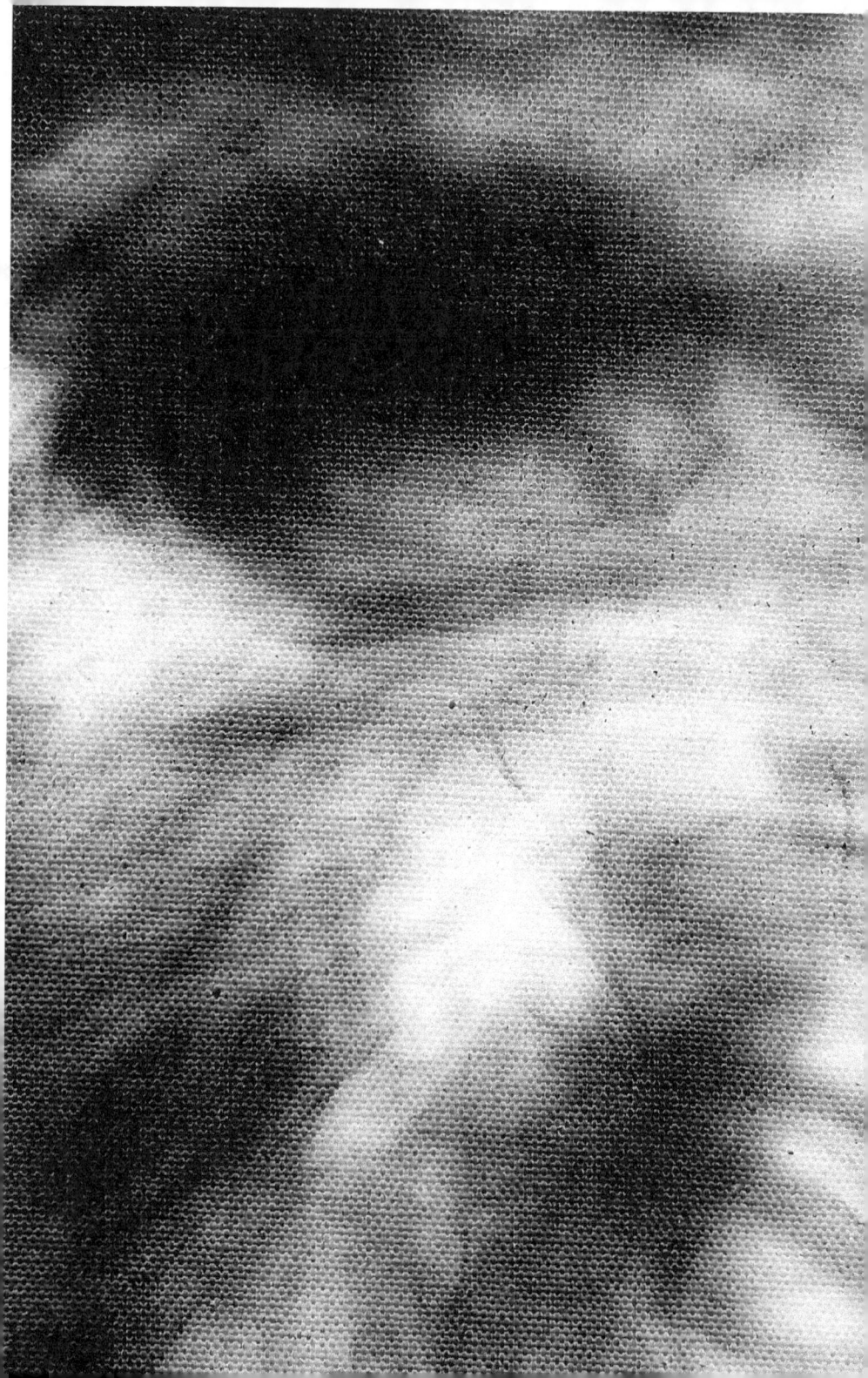

Ethan Nosanow Levin

THE RABBIS & THE MOHICAN STORYTELLER

A Mohican storyteller told me
A Dakota woman would walk for
three days
to give birth at Bdote
    seventeen thousand Dakota grandmothers and grandfathers,
    women and children
    marched after the war from the
    Western frontier
    To *two-and-a-half* acres in the
    valley there
    every day
    three to four would die
the soldiers would descend the hillside
to collect the dead
When the grandmothers and
grandfathers heard
the way their bodies had been treated
in Mankato
    They buried their own
        in the mud under the
        fire

The rabbis told me that a man named Akiva
Left his wife to live in squalor
so he could read a book in the
wilderness and
return a wealthy man
he declared Bar Kokhba the Messiah
- not Jesus of Nazarene -
Because Bar Kokhba fought for the
people. then,
    amidst the death throes of a
    world that would shake Akiva
    into confidence
    that a man could save a people
    and a land from its own
    composure
To survive among the other and
return a wealthy man

It was a wealthy man, said the Mohican
storyteller, who corrupted and named corruption
for himself, the names of our homestead,
Ramsey and Sibley
    they propagated the roots a
    decade earlier
    for the tree that would bear fruit a
    decade later
They would harvest to the benefit of the Nations
to the detriment of its leaves.

And the rabbis still teach
of Akiva and his wealth of Torah and
of his insistence to study
    Upon pain of death by Turnus Rufus
    upon the impression of pins and needles
    He was able to let leave his lips
    the last call to listen

Adonai echad

The Mohican told of the wife of Akiva, who
planted four trees too close by
    so their canopy enmeshed, upon his
    death
These were cut down a century and a half later
To be planted on Church grounds

And there is a concentration camp under the
aqueducts
And harmony at Golgotha

Where we began to be haunted
By the ghosts in our own shadow

We extended it even further, stretching the last
gasp of the sun so
we may live in its light for one more day
Before returning to its study
    To find the signs of Her return

To feel the birth of the white buffalo

That does not transcend

But happened in this place
At this time
Where I stand.

PROLOGUE TO HALAKHAH & AGGADAH

Q: Which normative world do you inhabit?
　　　From which reality do you rest from waking
　　　Remember to shake, and conclude
　　　Upon yourself, the permission to actualize
　　　A personhood, of a casuistic nature

Q: And which comes first, the person, place, or time?
　　　One says from the second
　　　And then does with each
　　　God, one
　　　Halakhah, second
　　　Aggadah, each

Q: And from which to ask questions to narrate?
　　　The Law cannot exist without it
　　　Story creates the nature
　　　To ultimately describe
　　　A nomos separate from narration

Q: And how do you constitute yourself against the other?
　　　Becomes the question unbecoming
　　　By which you might prescribe
　　　A death away from the sight of sacrality
　　　Which occurs only itself
　　　As if there is a self without the other
　　　As if Halakhah begs Aggadah
　　　And Aggadah were a ruinous mill which previously
　　　Churned our performance in hymnity

CAPITAL & COLONIAL

So where do Walter Benjamin and the apostle Paul find
common ground?
    In witness
           to the Jew within & the Indian without
compiling a string of quotations to describe a world
      which they keep at arm's length
a male prophet to the gentiles fed up with history
& its calamities
knowing all evidence already existed for human catastrophe
to make the case that no more evidence was required.

So abandon the human! choose only the self
    If our only point of connection is in evolution, then conceive
of yourself as master of your creation and seek to be sufficient
as such.

It has only been a matter of time since human connection
has felt so female
      but instead of rejecting it
          I embrace her
              and apologize
         And she says
             "thank me instead."

I'm sorry for the books that I would save from fire,
for trying to understand those who write living degrees of wonder
I find myself wanting, so what do you perform?
                    capital & colonial

THE REBBE FLEW

from rome to dc the rebbe flew ::
      owing to the roots that create wreckage as much as they create
he shifted from speaking the language of saints to bishops

                a fish the size of ten brooklyn blocks
                        :: flattened queens
                    it was rebuilt as amazon city

a wave rose up to meet the rebbe as he crossed the circum-atlantic
      as tall as the twin towers and as opaque as *ima shalom* ::
who would discuss his fear of god

:: in amazon city, there ran upon the shipment centers the son of lilith,
                                  written by men
      a school-shooter-type devil-child alt-right-troll
he was allowed to continue in this manner until his word was reached
                                by further study

when the rebbe came back to crown heights, Elijah and him
walked to the water
      where *ziz sadai* the griffin stood in a turbulent bottomless bay ::
who quickly befriended and estranged leviathan and behemoth as
one would family

goose fat was known to flood the sewers of amazon new york
and sporadically light on fire
so the city called the eternal-repair-man ::

who at long last, having failed to find any meaning,
returned to work

Ethan Nosanow Levin   :

Pompeia Plotina

Pompeia Plotina – an epicurean,
lashing upon the senate for its excesses
who harbors all the poetry of *kyrios* in her womb, for she gave
birth on the ninth of av, and the child
died on hannukah, and

her grief interminable
present alone
the grammar dictates her fury
towards the thrust of
war that is the game of hollow others
which envisions herself a creation gone wrong
as if to be created without meaning
is as to sin, so that she became
in mourning
part lilith, written by men and
part shekhinah, persistently captured in catch & release
that when the politicians came
and told of the latent kike
who lamented at her penultimate joy
and lit candles for her greatest sorrow, and so

she wrote to trajan of their absent yield,
so that he might reap
souls for the nourishing of
void & chaotic names

and descend upon the few
as a swift and taloned bird
with all its royal and predatory guise
upon which requisite sufferers might hold in them the
thrust of empire
finally compromising
total integrity of being.
in true grace
she brought trajan to those rabbis within five days
(when without his spirit it would have been double)
and found them obsessed in study
surrounding them with the piles of those consequences
he told the centurions to strike

Ethan Nosanow Levin   :

The Latent Kike

knowingly, father
i was raised like you ... or as those around me, i swear
only to find i was a jew
upon this latest rupture
here i am, eyes rye to encounter
alone in a plot-twist hell-hole; hanging with dull and
nauseous inconsistencies

i go out and walk sometimes; i live at bdote, north
there is a graveyard *kittim, goyim* close by
i walk there sometimes, and talk to the spirits of a stray ghost
they tell me of the jewish burial site across the way
which is locked and open only upon demand from the living,
so i remain there; i tell a quorum of pioneers about the election

karl krist kempf (1805-1862) would come to boast
(regardless of the leader of the free world)
the jewish burial site across the way would remain locked
until upon demand from the living, so that the dead could not visit
the souls of those buried there would idle in isolation;
the pandemic quarantined them away from their ancestors

election night i scaled the iron gate surrounding
the temple of aaron cemetery
and found elijah tending the souls there, saying
"it is best not your intention to learn your torah here;
i know of the world of the living, the dead are better left with me
if you pretend to be a jew you are not
suffering along will be as if one always becoming"
and i still found myself wanting, father

A Cuckold Agriculture

CRASH the door
Splits open and out CRAWLS
Four goat-heads, eyes RYE to encounter
The asphalt of EXISTENCE, satan's wry smile
But were it not for satan who would have TOLD Sarah
About Abraham binding Isaac; He slew her with TRUTH
At this POINT, standing face to the face with the devil freshly reaped
I was forced to say nothing, and meet her at the level of EQUAL exchange
On which her HOUSE was built; stored below lay a plot of anthropes and thistles.
Where blinding yellow hair sunk UNDER the comprehension of the blueness of her eyes
Shown to the stars as a RAY of resultant inoculation for deepest memories of daft meadows
In hymnity, she inspired the submergence of a CUCKOLD agriculture upon the banks of the Da

Ethan Nosanow Levin   :

A Lament of the Talmudic Page

לאלאלאלאלאלאל לאלאלא   לאלאלאלאלאלאל לאלאלא
אלאלאלאללאל אלאללא אלאלאא   אלאלאלאללאל אלאללא אלאלאא
ללאלל אלאלאלאלאלא לאלא לאלא‐   ללאלל אלאלאלאלאלא לאלא לאלא
ללאלאלללאלאלאלאלאלאלאלללאלאלאלאלאלאל לאלל   ללאלאלללאלאלאלאלאלאלאלללאלאלאלאלאלאל לאלל
ללאלאלאלאלאלאלאל   אלא אל אלללא לא   ללאלאלאלאלאלאלאל אלא אל אלללא לא
ללא אאלללא לאאא לאלאלאלאל אלא‐   ללא אאלללא לאאא לאלאלאלאל אלא‐
לאל אלאלאללא לאל לאלאל אלאל אל   לאל אלאלאללא לאל לאלאל אלאל אל לאלאלאלאל
לאלאלאל אלל לולואלאלאל ל   אל אל לאלאלאל ל אל אל לאלאלאל ל לולואלאלאל אלל לולואלאלאל ל

לאלאלא אלאלא	stand up you and protest to god	לאלא אלאלא
לאלא אלאלא	you interject with thesae adjecverbs and	אלאלא לאלא
אלאלא לאלא	excremondiments thos it is not wtihuot	לאלא אלאלא
לאלא אלאלא	flowers whenth plumes of scentlde dust	אלאלא לאלא
אלאלא לאלא	of sylvan matter which is ultimately a	לאלא אלאלא
לאלא אלאלא	story of two ovens	אלאלא לאלא
אלאלא לאלא	akhnai or auschwitz; a goring of	לאלא אלאלא
לאלא אלאלא	endodissentertainment and a history of	אלאלא לאלא
אלאלא לאלא	excommunisticdisclassificassociationism	לאלא אלאלא
לאלא אלאלא	which here expressed on the page	אלאלא לאלא
אלאלא לאלא	engauges or esqualifies itself	לאלא אלאלא

לאלאלאלאלאלאל לאלאלא   לאלאלאלאלאלאל לאלאלא
אלאלאלאללאל אלאללא אלאלאא   אלאלאלאללאל אלאללא אלאלאא
ללאלל אלאלאלאלאלא לאלא לאלא‐   ללאלל אלאלאלאלאלא לאלא לאלא‐
ללאלאלללאלאלאלאלאלאלאלללאלאלאלאלאלאל לאלל   ללא
ללאלאלאלאלאלאלאל אלא אל אלללא לא   ללאלאלאלאלאלאלאל אלא אל אלללא לא
ללא אאלללא לאאא לאלאלאלאל אלא‐   ללא אאלללא לאאא לאלאלאלאל אלא‐
לאל אלאלאללא לאל לאלאל אלאל אל   לאל אלאלאללא לאל לאלאל אלאל אל אל
לאלאלאל אלל לולואלאלאל ל   לאלאלאל ל אלאלאלאל ל לולואלאלאל אלל לולואלאלאל ל

הבאת עד נבכי–ים? ובחקר תהום התהלכת? הנגלו לך שערי–מות? ושערי צלמות
(תראה? התבננת עד רחבי–ארץ? הגד אם ידעת כלה. (איוב ל"ח:ט"ז-י"ט

NOTES

"The Rabbis & the Mohican Storyteller"

Bdote is the Dakota word for the area surrounding the intersection of the Minnesota and Mississippi rivers, and it is the site of genesis for the Dakota people. The white colonizers stationed the military outpost, Fort Snelling, in the valley above Bdote. After the 1862 US-Dakota War, 17,000 Dakota elders, women, and children were forcibly marched from the Western frontier of the territory of Minnesota to a concentration camp at Bdote. The surviving male soldiers were imprisoned at Mankato, where over 330 were sentenced to death. Abraham Lincoln pardoned most of them but for the sake of Native-government relations nationwide. The bodies of the 38 that were hung were stolen from their mass grave. One of the skulls ended up on the desk of the founder of the Mayo Clinic. The story of the Dakota people and their creation and suffering at Bdote was told to me by Mohican storyteller, Reverend Jim Bear Jones, during a sacred sites tour organized by the Minnesota Council of Churches.

The story of Rabbi Akiva leaving his wife is found in Bavli Ketubot 62b-63a. The report of Rabbi Akiva making messianic claims about Bar Kokhba is found in Yerushalmi Ta'anit 68d. The martyrdom of Rabbi Akiva is found in Bavli Berakhot 61b.

"Prologue to Halakhah & Aggadah"

Engaging the philosophical formulation of Halakhah & Agga-
dah by Hayyim Nachman Bialik: Bialik, Hayyim N. "Halakhah
and Aggadah or Law and Lore" in *Revealment and Concealment:
Five Essays* (Jerusalem: Ibis Editions, 2000), 45-87.

"Capital & Colonial"

Capital is the Halakhah. Colonial is the Aggadah.

"The Rebbe Flew"

"The Rebbe Flew" is a reference to how Rebbe Menachem Men-
del Schneerson, the leader of the Chabad dynasty of Chasidism,
never travelled to Israel for fear of bringing about the end of
days. He is still considered by some in Chabad to be the Messiah,
despite his passing in 1993.

This poem is a poetic gloss on the story cycle of fantastic crea-
tures in Bavli Bava Batra 73a-b.

Ima Shalom was the wife of Rabbi Eleazar ben Hyrcanus. He
was excommunicated by his fellow rabbis for his ruling on the
oven of Akhnai, despite being supported directly by God. She
was also the sister of Rabban Gamaliel, who said fraudulent
things about her husband and voted to excommunicate him. Ima
Shalom attempted to prevent her husband from praying to God,
lest his prayers bring about the death of her brother because of
his fraudulent words. During the new moon, a poor man came
to beg for food at the house of Ima Shalom, and while she was
distracted, Rabbi Eleazar ben Hyrcanus prostrated himself and
caused the death of her brother through his lament. The story
of the oven of Akhnai can be found in Bavli Bava Batra 59a-b.

The idea of "Amazon City," a dystopian world where large tech companies become like nation-states, is derived from Alexis Pauline Gumbs collection M Archive, where they discuss the "Google kingdom": Gumbs, Alexis Pauline. *M Archive* (Durham: Duke University Press, 2018).

"Pompeia Plotina"

Based on a story found in the late antique midrashic collections, Esther Rabbah and Eichah Rabbah. I include an English translation of the original story below:

And the third was in the days of Trajan, may his bones be crushed! His wife gave birth on the night of the Ninth of Av, and all Israel was mourning. The child died on Hannukah. Israel said: 'Will we light or will we not light the Hannukah candles?' They said: 'We will light, and all that happens will happen.' So they lit. And the people went to speak wrong of the Jews to the wife of Trajan, saying: 'Those Jews, when you gave birth, they were mourning, and when the child died, they lit their wicks.' She sent and wrote to her husband: 'While you've been suppressing the Barbarians, the Jews have rebelled against you. Come and suppress them.' Trajan boarded a ship, and thought to come in 10 days, but there was a wind and he came in 5 days. He came and uncovered the Jews engaged in the learning of this verse: "The Lord will lift upon you a nation from remoteness, from the extremity of space, like the vulture swoops down..." (Deut 28:49) Trajan said to them: 'I am he, the vulture who thought to come in ten days and was given by the wind in five days.' He surrounded them with his legions, and he slew them. (Esther Rabbah Petichta 1:3, my translation)

Pompeia Plotina, the historical wife of Trajan, was a noted Epicurean. She was famous for advocating for the reduction of excess in the senate.

"The Latent Kike"

Kittim is a word for Gentiles, particularly the Greeks, found in Jeremiah 2:10, Ezekiel 27:6, and throughout the Dead Sea Scrolls. Goyim literally means nations but has become a derogatory term for non-Jews.

1805 is the year the first treaty was signed between the Dakota and the US government. The treaty was only signed by two non-ranking members of the Dakota but was still ratified by the government. The US-Dakota War and subsequent concentration camps, mass murder, and exile of the Dakota took place in 1862.

"A Cuckold Agriculture"

A midrash tells of how Satan, attempting to thwart Abraham doing God's bidding, pushes the knife from Abraham's hand as he is about to sacrifice Isaac. At this point, the angel calls to Abraham to stop the sacrifice. If Satan had not done this, Abraham would have sacrificed Isaac. Satan also disguised himself as Isaac and told Sarah about God's order to Abraham to sacrifice Isaac. He had hardly completed relating the news when Sarah fainted and died of grief. See Midrash Tanchuma, Vayera 23.

"Lament of the Talmudic Page"

Evokes the format commonly used in printings of the Talmud and other Jewish books, which includes the primary text centered in the middle with commentary formatted along either side. The Hebrew phonetically sounds like "lalala," but those two letters combined have a variety of meanings.

The oven of Akhnai references the story of Ima Shalom, Rabbi Eliezar ben Hyrcanus, and Rabban Gamaliel mentioned under the notes for "The Rebbe Flew."

The two quotes at the bottom of the page are from Job 38:16-19, and from the story of the oven of Akhnai in Bavli Bava Batra 59b, mentioned above:

Have you penetrated to the sources of the sea, or walked in the recesses of the abyss? Have the gates of death been disclosed to you? Have you seen the gates of deep darkness? Have you surveyed the expanses of the earth? If you know of these—tell Me. (Job 38:16-18, JPS translation)

The Gemara relates that generations later Rabbi Natan met the Prophet Elijah. Rabbi Natan asked Elijah about the debate between Rabbi Eliezer and Rabbi Yehoshua [who argued on the side of Rabban Gamaliel.] He said to him: "What did the holy one, blessed be He, do at that time when Rabbi Yehoshua refused to heed the heavenly voice [and ruled against Rabbi Eliezer ben Hyrcanus]? In reply, Elijah said to Rabbi Natan: "God smiled and said: 'My sons have defeated Me, My sons have defeated Me!'" (Bavli Bava Batra 59b, Steinsaltz translation and commentary)

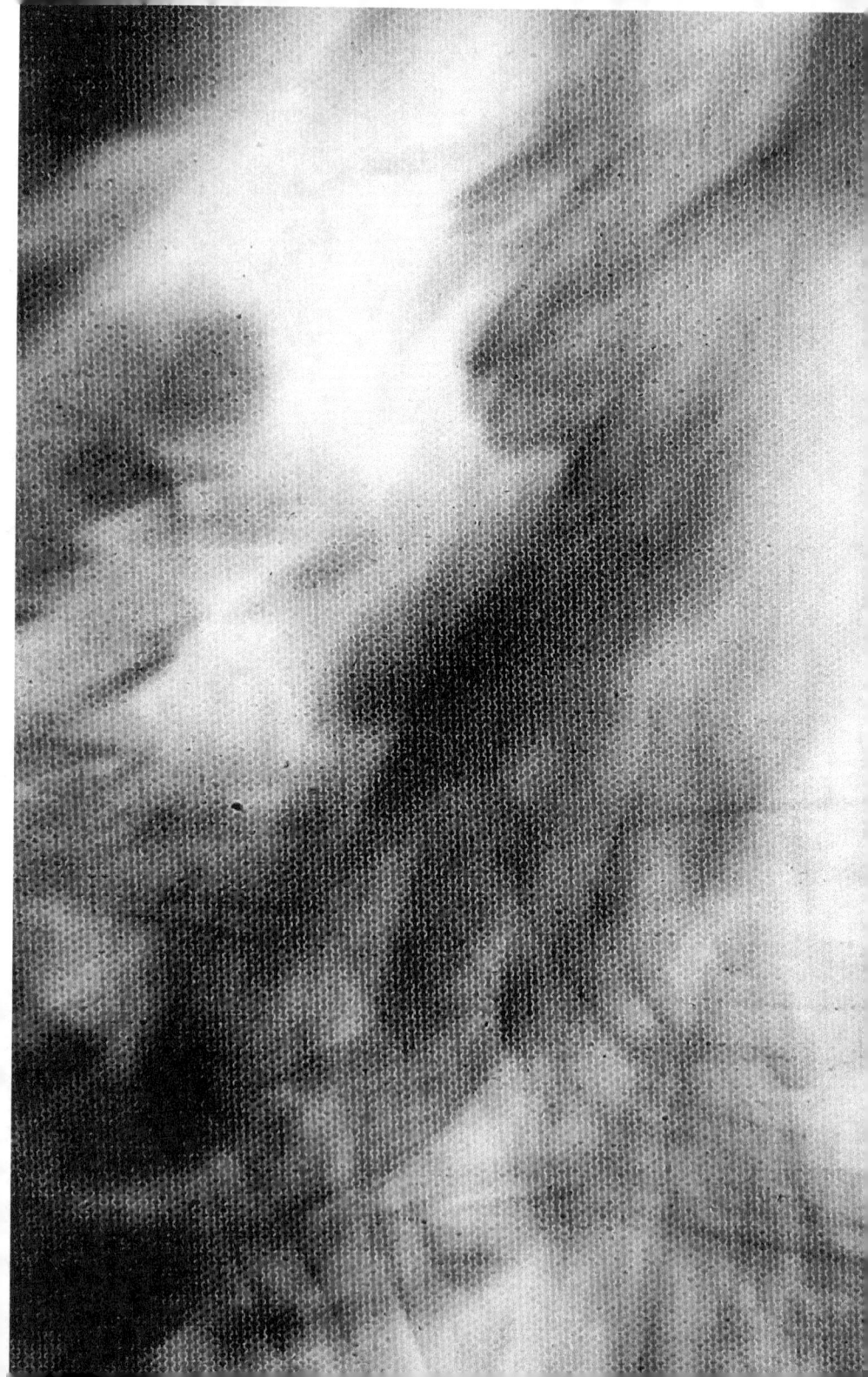

∴ Abigail Grace Louisin ∴

YELLOW

The memory starts first
as a color I hear,
a hum, a wicker basket

lifted from the grass,
leaves painted happy by the wind.
        It is ripe light pouring

and pooling on a blanket,
        holding us between breaths
her whispering prayers in the shape of a fig.

IN GUSTS / IN GHOSTS

dirt pale knuckles clutch a small life to a bony chest   a single
shoe in the desert   the prophet's ashes blow in gusts / in ghosts
over sands   a shadow of a woman crouches in the thistles   lily
of the valley   beneath a bloodless mortal sun   that smolders
we wait   anointed in oil   *holy in our pain and holy in Name*   we
are still waiting   a saguaro began to look like my father seven
days ago   I wonder when it will finish   they say *no estás se-*
gura but when have I ever been safe   I feel safe when I forget
I am figured like woman   like Eve   like Lilith   I am told
that bad things happen because of me   we are not the chosen
ones   but if we pray and trust in the phantom promise of Ca-
naan then maybe we will remember   God   maybe one day they
will remember that we died in the shifting dunes of the desert
a black bird landed on my father's shoulders and stared at me
with one eye, told me: *never forget the kings, the exile, the whispers*

GRIEF IN GLASS [SHAPE]

Shimmer clinks   glass
        on the brink of the world
Let the shards lodge

Fingers in my mouth
Pull me out from myself

I ink
the page dry
scatter my own ashes,
Let them
        sink
                deeper than
                        grief

THE WORLD ENDS IN A CHARCOAL SKETCH

The scan is a charcoal sketch,
smoked cave with tumors alight.
In white like the beach I will find you on,
in the after.

I cannot separate my sadness from yours;
I cannot speak of the space that will be ours.
Cruelty, after all, is made of distance.

NOWHERE GOLD

I ask my father where he goes sometimes.
In the midst of the life that is ours now,
a vacancy in his body and oceaned eyes
no longer rippling. There are no waves
where he goes. I wave *hello* afraid
this is our last haunt again.

He is back. He smiles
not enough to convince me
that wherever he went is nowhere.

I wish I had his gift: to disappear into a forest.
A single tree. Trace the gold rings
like I trace his wedding band. Rooted.
I want to go somewhere in the middle of nowhere
and be nothing and instead be something
someone admires from a photograph.
Visit me in November when I have lost my leaves.
When I am all that is left.

They gave my mother six months to live. I smile
through telling my loved ones that I am okay.
I go to my somewhere that is nowhere

and think of myself wearing her rings when she dies,
which she will, probably before next fall. I write
these words and they feel as real as nowhere.
Tree of me with gold leaves like fire
and a trunk unbroken halve.

& *or*
[AN AMPERSAND AS A WOMAN] I

an ampersand [a woman],
Curled inward,
Pulled outward.
Two things at once.

She is clay   water,
Made by the river,

Weighed down by the river,

"Wait [& wade]
down by the river."

& *or*
[AN AMPERSAND AS A WOMAN] II

italicized,
she leans right,
she pulls light,
she breaks waves
crashing, white
and the water trickles
over parts of herself
    [of myself]

we forget on purpose

inked asterisk
on cracking waves
splashing light
down & into
our body.

FALLING ROOKS LIKE TEARS

Not salt but sand
    human delight (we)
        forget we are grieving
    falling like rooks cawing in air

      forget gravity's pull
      spindling feathers
curved shells, transparent
      carnelian clouds
      and lapping waves

Which do you notice first— the wave or the sea?

Not mourning but salt
    human forgetting (we)
        delight in our falling
air cawing, carnelian
rooks
    spindling gravity
       transparent feathers
waves grieving, curved
      clouds
      mother of pearl
      and other broken shells

           we are both wave and sea
           and this is our work

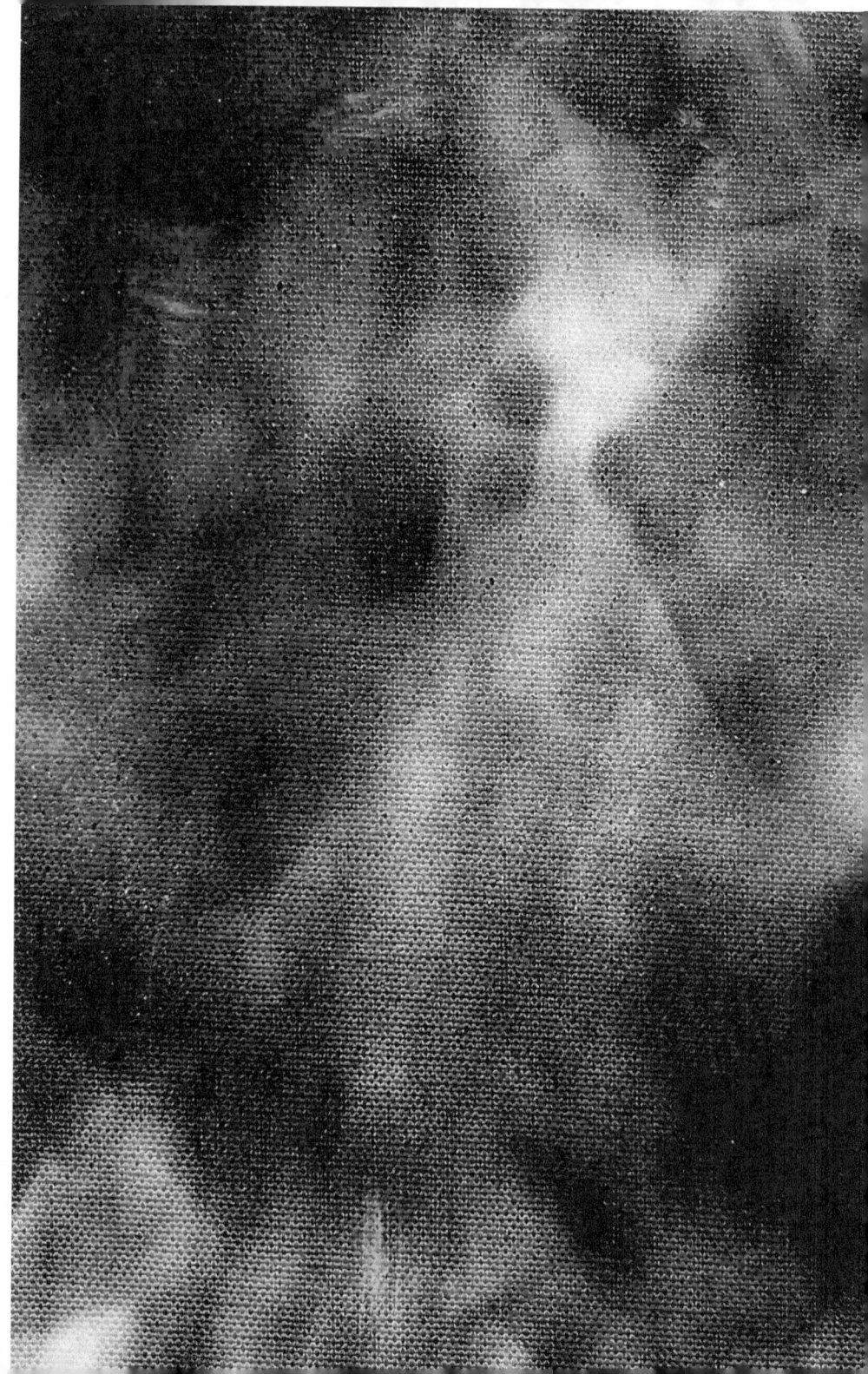

Jason Adam Sheets

November of Quietly Children

Notes of leafrot and husk feed an eye-birch-triple of a thing.

've a river in hand.
You've a wreath of tombs, combs, honeycombs—

An arcanum tick of hot honey
under a birthmarked moon
here soon.

Premised by a flake of rose on pale grass, the cherry spark
of a laureate's crown defrosts.

Here, the ghost rests beneath a silent shoe. Something of an orange
flower of a swollen hour; a marble eye-
lid of discontent limed
to good cups.

You paint musical wool with a trembling paw.
I build castles of pipes on ropes of sand.

A cage of snow licks salt from scissor and skin
and the tongue: a candle, a candle in arms (the flame in the shape of a block).

A link rings alive through oblivion's red window.
I sense the hissing azaleas, barefoot on notes of leafrot and husk.

JANUS

I tune to an hourglass at the bottom of the sea.

Beneath the waves, the glass sings a sufferable harmony—
that like the thinning of the human face,
that like my ghost, who sings all of his minutes away.

[The long table knows his last great aloneness.]

He once built a ship for a woman at the foot of a mountain of scrying monke

a ship in two places
twin stars of an equal birth
named—

In a dream,
I find the mountain and steal the name of the ship back from him.

The face of the man is never the face of the man who faces two places.
He is only deep enough when he is face down among hours,
caught in the hand like a dead clock in water.

THE FISHERMAN (OMEN)

A string of stone beads
is plucked from the sea
by the fisherman home
in his mirrored abyss.

A cradle of turnings
in an energetic wake pools
then sinks—

To catch the true nature
of one's omen:

Position a libation. Pour.

Prize the catch
(like a vessel of fish)
plucked backward
from the wink of the arch.

Unmoored, tell cold.

Magnetic Room

By what rains do I—

    the [telling] clock in the tide
    the [telling] structure of ash
    the [telling] horn beneath windowglass

A wave swells toward me

                            or not—

but I am in a room and from the sideways slant of this yellow
corner can see the wilted leaf cherrying, the spoon in the bowl,
how the three seem to halve themselves from my vision or have
themselves I do not know if one made thing can own another
and I wonder if I could complete another living thing I mean
compete with no I mean complete—I look out of the window's
windowglass a wave swells toward me carrying with it a story
that beg-ends with a circular thud twice dissolved in the eye of
some living thing and O by what rains do I *I* and why didn't I
know you   when I was alive.

Seven

in a pure dent of its shade

a tinny hook mirrors in slow spin

weaving a thunderstone lock of the mouth

needle needling needless need needy needles needlelike

the little keyed whorls seven a crispness

seven the (curious) knots of brittle crosses

pinned savage to their blazing yellow selves

THIEF IN THE REEDS

thunder thumps
the ashy river alive

and the tempest of the cold
beige breaks into me

a field of poppies
lavender or sapphire

and eyes of an apple's heart—
a horse licks the living core

and scattering off he scatters
me soft to the thief in the reeds

A Match Can Become a Witch
If a Child Makes It So

She pilfers a patch of cornflowers.
She carries a storm in her mother's eye.

    She is the thing that moves through trees,
    in shock of the seed pointing downward.

She takes a bloodstone from her pocket,
skips it across a sleeping lake.

Across the lake, fireweed rings a burning trunk,
a transient grove of electric story:

    The fire fell from the claw of the bird with many masks.
    On a ritual mask, the mouth can be omitted.

A fish belongs to the lake.
A fish her father was never able to eat.

The fish's gaze hangs in the air like a paper banner—

    Did you know you can harness the energy of a cloud
    if you pluck the eyes from the fingers of the nun
    whose face is a window?

Breton saw a man cut in two by the window.
The man was a fish seeking thunder in piles of sticks.

    She learned to count the sticks ...

and pomegranates: fruit's frequent potential:
the space within seeds is measured by need.

    She sails through the strings of a harp, her apparition.

She jumps into an eclipse off a cliff that becomes an arm—
See, she's died twice with seeds in her teeth-teeth-teeth.

STONEWARD

An origin spirit tucked in a tree-
hollow flits with an elemental
hunger for the fruit of a seed.
Red unthreads from its wrist
as an auric garden reveals
its landscape: igneous stone
stairs cooled to a smooth slide.
In the distance, three shined
wooden boats pose vertical
on a paradisiacal sea as a bale
of young turtles tend wildly
to their visions. The red thread
on the cooled lava becomes a
freshet hurrying toward the sea
where there is no word for how
an ivory whelk lying on sand looks
when eyed through clear water.

THE MAKERS

The makers	ABRACADABRA
climb everlasting stalks	ABRACADABR
a glittery blue crop	ABRACADAB
of musical masts	ABRACADA
	ABRACAD
stone-folk of an æther	ABRACA
alone and fully real	ABRAC
	ABRA
their book written	ABR
in an aeon of twining	AB
is a spontaneous birth	A
of radiant keeping.	

They build their boat
from star to star
anchor to the antler
of Orion: an illustrious art

an abracadabra
and the core
the glassy core—

In an open eye
(fluent to matters)
one reads:

To unmake the world, find the center of a thought.

They are the authors
of a double unpeopling

the builders of shipwrecks
of tin-packed stars.

Virga

A hummingbird
flies backward
through a cave
of painted bulls
appearing only
when paused
in wet light.

A crown spider
crawls out of a hole
commanding rain—

vapor is a time
when all sound
becomes human

when the white eye of life

writes law on a feather
writes sin on an arrow

to middle the names carved
in the hidden.

NOTES

"JANUS"

In this poem, "JANUS" is the name of the ship, with the Janus-image attempting to enter Theseus's paradox through the "I," as inspired by the line, "And which ship is the image or impostor," from Dan Beachy-Quick's poem, "Theseus's Ship," in *Arrows*.

"A Match Can Become a Witch If a Child Makes It So"

This title is a paraphrase of a section of a paper on "the force of the daemonic world of childhood," written by ethnologist and archaeologist Leo Frobenius.

This poem is partly inspired by the many "seeds" and "fires" in Brian Teare's *Doomstead Days*.

"The Makers"

"To unmake the world, find the center of a thought," is borrowed from *The Dawning Moon of the Mind* by Susan Brind Morrow.

This poem is a mythopoetic response to *A Treatise on Stars* by Mei-mei Berssenbrugge.

About the Poets

.

Charli Pence Bond studied digital cinema and creative writing at DePaul University, and received a Master of Theological Studies from Harvard Divinity School. She currently is a writer and reporter for *The Daily Wire* and her work has been published in *The Washington Times, The Federalist, Glamour* magazine, and journals associated with the University of Oxford. She is the author of *Where You Go* (Center Street, 2018) as well as three children's books her mother illustrated (Regnery Kids). She lives with her wildly encouraging and adventurous husband who serves in the U.S. Navy.

:

Ethan Nosanow Levin is a Master of Theological Studies candidate at Harvard Divinity School, concentrating in Jewish Studies. As an undergraduate, his scholarship centered on Jewish hermeneutics of imperialism in the Midrash. As a graduate student, his research has shifted to the relationship between Jews and colonialism, with an upcoming presentation on Minnesotan Jews and coloniality being given at the 25th Western Jewish Studies conference in Spring 2021. In addition, Levin's sexual violence prevention work with high school and college football players has been nationally recognized.

∴

Abigail Grace Louisin is a Master of Theological Studies candidate at Harvard Divinity School, concentrating in Women, Gender, Sexuality, and Religion. As a graduate student, she is interested in women's religious experiences throughout the Americas, poetry and the lyric essay, death and dying, and the body. While studying Religion and English as an undergraduate at Baldwin Wallace University, she was awarded the A.W. Bud Collins Jr. Scholarship for Creative Writing. Her most recent publications can be found in *The Mill* (2019, 2020). Abigail is forever indebted to the love and grace of her family and loved ones and is particularly thankful for Professors Sharon Kubasak and Ellen Posman for their years of encouragement and red ink.

∷

Jason Adam Sheets holds a Master of Theological Studies degree from Harvard Divinity School. He is the author of *A Madness of Blue Obsidian* (2022) and *The Hour Wasp* (2017) and is the recipient of the 2016 Poetry Society of New Hampshire Poetry Prize. His poems have appeared in numerous journals and magazines and have most recently been featured by The Oxford Research Centre in the Humanities and *The Graduate Journal of Harvard Divinity School*. He has taught in Harvard's Poetry in America for High Schools Program and has worked as a mentor for AWP's writer to writer mentorship program. His work has been supported by Harvard University, PEN America, and Poets & Writers.